YOSEMITE

BY
Lorraine Jolian Cazin

I wish to thank Leonard McKenzie, Chief Park Interpreter of Yosemite National Park, for all his help.

PUBLISHED BY

CRESTWOOD HOUSE
Mankato, MN, U.S.A.

CIP

LIBRARY OF CONGRESS CATALOGING IN PUBLICATION DATA

Cazin, Lorraine Jolian.
  Yosemite

  (National parks)
  Includes index.
  SUMMARY: Describes the geography and animal life of Yosemite National Park, with a discussion of how it became a national park.
  1. Natural history — California — Yosemite National Park — Juvenile literature. 2. Yosemite National Park (Calif.) — Juvenile literature.
[1. Natural history — California — Yosemite National Park. 2. Yosemite National Park (Calif.) 3. National parks and reserves.] I. Title.
II. Series: National parks (Mankato, Minn.)
QH105.C2C39   1988   508.794'47—dc19   88-20236
ISBN 0-89686-407-3

International Standard Book Number:	Library of Congress Catalog Card Number:
0-89686-407-3	88-20236

PHOTO CREDITS

Cover: DRK Photo: Lewis Kemper
DRK Photo: (Gary R. Zahm) 4, 9; (Lewis Kemper) 18-19, 30-31; (Larry Ulrich)
  21; (Pat O'Hara) 25, 38-39
Bill Allen: 6, 13, 14-15, 16, 22, 23
Journalism Services: (Jerry Ward) 11, 26; (James F. Quinn) 32, 34-35
Tom Stack: (John Gerlach) 27, 28, 36, 41, 42-43

Produced by Carnival Enterprises.

CRESTWOOD·HOUSE

Box 3427, Mankato, MN, U.S.A. 56002

TABLE OF CONTENTS

Yosemite National Park

VISITORS IN THE PARK

In 1987, more than three million people visited Yosemite National Park in California. Many came from all over the United States. Others came from lands around the world. They had heard of Yosemite's waterfalls and had read about Yosemite's landmarks.

The visitors came to explore and examine all 761,757 acres. They rode the free shuttle buses, rented horses and bikes, and hiked many of the park's 800 miles of trails. They temporarily became amateur *ecologists*—people who study our earth and all living things.

Some spent a day, others a week. Some came alone, some with their families, or with a school tour. They stayed in tent-cabins, lodges, cottage rooms, camp housekeeping units, or in hotels.

They came to see the black bears, and saw some of the park's bird and mammal species, 11 species of fish, and 29 species of amphibians and reptiles.

They came to see sequoias and some of its 1,400 flower species.

They camped, swam, fished, boated, backpacked, and rock climbed.

They took in all the sights, photographed the views, wrote postcards home about their adventures, and bought souvenirs to remind them of their California vacation.

Yosemite Falls and one of Yosemite's meadows provide a perfect setting for a picnic.

WHAT IS A NATIONAL PARK?

Years ago, Europe's wealthy people set land aside for their own enjoyment. Whenever they wanted, they could walk, picnic, ride, or hunt on their own land. The poor and middle class people, however, had no such open spaces.

The founders of the United States wanted things to be different here. And in 1864, something happened that gave all people a place to go, no matter how much money they had. Congress passed an act granting to California the areas of Yosemite called "Yosemite Valley" and the Mariposa Grove.

Thousand-year-old sequoia trees grow in Yosemite's Mariposa Grove.

Soon after came the idea of national parks. In 1890, Congress created four national parks, including Yosemite. A national park is public land with unusual beauty. It should have unique wildlife. It should have something special that no other park has. And Congress must pass a law setting the land aside so that it is a protected area.

Yosemite belongs as much to the people of Minnesota, New York, or Florida as to those who live in Nevada and California. It belongs to every citizen in the United States.

National parks are popular and attract many visitors. But too many visitors can cause problems. Yosemite is one of the most popular national parks in the country. It is open 24 hours a day, 365 days of the year. It is rarely closed. In summer, people have a hard time finding a place to stay. Many trails are overused and clogged with hikers.

At one time, park officials talked about banning cars from the valley floor. But they soon realized that there was not enough land for buildings and parking lots.

To solve some of these problems in the early 1970s, the park created one-way road traffic patterns. People were not allowed to drive their cars in the east end of the valley. Instead, tourists were provided with free transportation in the valley and in Mariposa Grove.

After five years of study and suggestions made by many people, the Yosemite General Management Plan (GMP) was adopted in 1980. This plan guides the development of the park. It has become a model for many other national parks to follow.

Roads and parking lots have been improved. Trails have been made accessible for the disabled, and one and a half miles of electrical powerlines have been hidden underground.

YOSEMITE'S EARLY HISTORY

More than 2,000 years ago, Native Americans lived in the area of Yosemite National Park. At one time, there were many villages in the valley.

The people were primarily from the Southern Miwok tribes. The Miwok tribe developed a culture rich in religion, tradition, music, and politics. They called the valley "Ahwahnee," meaning "place of the gaping mouth." The name Yosemite came from the Miwok word "uzaumati," meaning "grizzly

FUN FACT Yosemite Park covers 1,190 miles and is about the size of the state of Rhode Island.

bear." Another tribe was the Mono Lake Paiute. They, like the Miwok, are still living in the area today.

In 1833, explorer Joseph Walker and his party became the first non-Indian people to come to the brink of Yosemite Valley.

The first-known entry into the valley was nearly 20 years later. Gold was discovered in 1849 in the Sierra Nevada foothills. Many miners came to make their fortunes. Fights began between the miners and the Native Americans who were trying to protect their homeland. Because of this, the Mariposa Battalion (a volunteer fighting force) was sent by the state of California in 1851 to bring an end to the Mariposa Indian War.

People slowly became aware of Yosemite Valley. Poets, authors, and artists arrived and were inspired by Yosemite. Their work spread news of the valley's beauty throughout the United States and the world.

People arrived on foot, on horseback, and by stagecoach. Houses were built, hotels were contructed. Orchards were planted, and livestock was brought into the meadows.

The year 1856 marked the visit of the first white woman, Madame Gautier. She liked the area and decided to stay. She became a housekeeper in the Mariposa Hotel. The next year, two San Francisco female teachers arrived. After this, observed a pioneer in the area, it was normal to see ladies in Yosemite.

Frederick Law Olmsted, the man who designed New York City's Central Park, noticed Yosemite's park-like character. He saw its nearly-level valley and the deep meadows of grass and flowers. He saw the *stands* of pines and *groves* of oaks.

He heard, too, that people were starting to misuse the land. Mining and lumbering companies preferred that Yosemite not be a park. Sheepherders and cattlemen wanted the lands for grazing.

In order to stop the growing threat to the land, Olmsted and I. W. Raymond appealed to President Abraham Lincoln to deed Yosemite to California. In 1864, Congress enacted a law, which was then signed by Lincoln. This law granted Yosemite Valley and the Mariposa Grove to California as a public trust.

When Congress created four national parks 26 years later, Yosemite Park did not include Yosemite Valley or the Mariposa Grove. They were still under the control of the state of California. It was not until 1906 that California returned these areas to the federal government. They were added

In the 1850s, people first heard about the beauty of the Yosemite Valley.

to what we now call Yosemite National Park.

In 1984, Congress passed the California Wilderness Bill to protect 3.2 million acres in California as wilderness. Passage of this bill designated 89% of Yosemite as wilderness. Yosemite National Park was now part of the National Wilderness System.

NATURE CHANGES YOSEMITE

Five hundred million years ago, the area of the Sierra Nevada and the Central Valley of California was a great sea. Large amounts of silt, mud, and sand settled on the sea floor. As the layers pressed together, the pressure turned them into rock.

In time, forces within the earth's crust pushed these layers above the sea level. The land bent and folded into mountain ranges.

As the mountains rose, hot and soft rock called *magma* began to form beneath the mountain. The magma cooled, hardened, and formed granite. This granite became the Sierra Nevada. Weather and water wore away the top layer of *sedimentary rocks*. This *erosion* made rolling hills, broad valleys, and winding streams.

The land continued to rise. It bent and twisted over much of eastern California and western Nevada. This made the western slopes steeper. This steepness increased the erosion, causing more mountainous land. The side streams were not touched and continued to flow. (This was because they tended to run in a north/south direction. As a result, their valleys were higher and higher above those streams.) In time, v-shaped canyons, some 2,000 feet deep, were carved into the landscape.

During the Ice Age, the earth's climate changed. It slowly grew very, very cold. Great amounts of snow and ice collected. *Glaciers* formed, advanced, and retreated. As they advanced, they picked up rocks in their path. These rocks scraped the earth. They were the cutting edges of the glaciers, both widening and deepening the canyons into U-shaped trenches.

Glaciers cut away the lower part of streams such as Yosemite Creek. This left valleys hanging even more steeply. Now streams flowed down the cliffs. In other places, ice cut great steps, leaving waterfalls in some areas and flat

FUN FACT When Queen Elizabeth II was going to visit California in 1983, she asked for a three-day vacation stopover to Yosemite. Her friends asked her, "Don't you want to see Hollywood?" She told them, "Perhaps, but most of all, I want to see Yosemite Valley."

valleys in others.

When the ice finally melted from the Sierra Nevada, it left behind Yosemite, a spectacular glacial valley.

Yosemite is still a very active geological area. In the future, *geologists* expect some major activity, perhaps an eruption, especially in the Mammoth Mountain area 40 miles southwest of Yosemite National Park.

THE MIWOK AND PAIUTE WHO LIVED ON THE LAND

The Miwok and Paiute people used almost all of the plants and animals in the Yosemite area for making food, clothing, or tools. They encouraged plants and grasses to grow back thicker and healthier. If lightning fires did not occur every year or two, they set the land on fire to clear away brush so new seedlings could grow. (Today, experts in forest management are just beginning to realize the value of small, controlled fires. They call it

Small, controlled fires clean out excess brush and provide room for new seedlings to grow.

"prescribed burning.")

There are still Miwok and Paiute people living in Yosemite. For a long time they were told to forget their old ways. Now some younger people are learning the ways of their forefathers.

Miwok and Paiute women made some of the finest baskets in the entire world. It could take as much as two and a half months, working four hours a day, to make one. Baskets supplied their household needs. They used them as pots, pans, canteens, sifters, packs, cradles, and drinking vessels. Young women were taught the art of basket weaving and practiced it all their lives.

The Native American Village in the valley has demonstrations during the summer of Native American basketry and cooking that show the cultural history of the Miwok. Tourists can see Native American artifacts (anything made by humans, especially a tool or weapon) such as baskets, ceremonial wear, arrowheads, and spear points.

JOHN MUIR

Some people call John Muir "the father of the national park idea." He devoted much of his life to the study of nature. He wrote about the importance of preserving the Sierra Nevada region. In the 1890s, he started the Sierra Club. He served as its president for 22 years until his death. Today, the Sierra Club is still active in conservation.

Muir was born in 1838 in Scotland. His family moved to a Wisconsin farm in 1849. At 22, he left home and roamed from city to city, taking any job he could get. He finally enrolled at the University of Wisconsin.

While working on a geology degree, he heard debates about how the Yosemite Valley was formed. Some people believed the valley evolved through floods, earthquakes, an act of God, or volcanic activity. Others were sure water and wind erosion, or lightning and *avalanches* played a role.

After two years, he left the University and headed for Yosemite. At first, he herded sheep and explored the mountain meadows. Then he got a job at a sawmill. He quit that for a job as a caretaker at a local hotel. During his hours off from work, he studied the evidence of glaciers through the valley and in the high country to the east. He believed the glaciers were involved in forming Yosemite.

In time, he discovered that glacial erosion was chiefly responsible for the

FUN FACT Dancing was a form of prayer for the Miwok and Paiute. Their fall Acorn Dance was performed in thanksgiving for their crops. They danced all day and all night for four days in a row. At the end of the dancing, they ate acorn mush and roasted venison.

The gigantic size of sequoia trees has amazed visitors for years.

creation of Yosemite Valley. This discovery led him to do even more studies of the Sierra Nevada Range.

In 1903, Muir asked President Theodore Roosevelt to come to Yosemite. He wanted to convince the President that the valley and Mariposa Grove should be added to Yosemite National Park. After a meal of unleavened biscuits and campfire-brewed coffee, the two bedded down in evergreen boughs among giant trunks of the sequoias. Muir and Roosevelt listened to the western hermit thrush and the sounds of waterfalls tumbling down the sheer cliffs. Roosevelt was impressed and agreed to support the idea of returning the valley and the grove to the federal government. Later Roosevelt wrote in a letter to a friend, "It was like being in a great solemn cathedral."

Muir left a message for all people. He told them to "Experience the wilderness…don't just read about it."

FUN FACT Photographing a giant sequoia is a challenge. Remember, one doesn't have to get the whole tree in the picture. Have someone stand next to it. This will give some idea of the tree's large size.

Mirror Lake reflects majestic mountains.

14

WHAT'S TO SEE AT YOSEMITE?

Yosemite has 761,757 acres of mountains and forests and 429 lakes. Lying on the western slope of the Sierra Nevada are two main canyons dividing the park from east to west: Yosemite Valley to the south and the Grand Canyon of the Tuolumne River to the north. A *canyon* is a narrow valley with high, steep sides, usually with a stream at the bottom.

Yosemite is crossed by a single road from the Big Oak Flat Entrance on the west to the Tioga Pass Entrance on the east. This road is closed in winter. Besides these entrances, there is the Arch Rock Entrance on the west that leads to Yosemite Valley. The South Entrance (Wawona Road) is near the Mariposa Grove of Giant Sequoias.

The park offers many areas of interest, including: Yosemite Valley, Glacier Point, Mariposa Grove of Big Trees, Badger Pass Ski Area, the Merced Lake area, Buck Camp area, and the White Wolf area. The largest area is Tuolumne Meadows in the northeastern corner of the park.

Most of the park's splendors are located in a seven-mile-long *gorge*. This deep, narrow valley is a mile wide and about 3,000 feet deep. It has sheer walls 2,000 to 4,800 feet high. Here are the Upper and Lower Yosemite Falls and the granite domes El Capitan and Half Dome.

Most visitors see this valley, but it is less than 1% of Yosemite National Park! Of the park's 1,190 square miles, this valley is only seven square miles. The reason so many people see just this area is that the major roads all lead into the valley.

It is possible to see the well-known attractions of the park such as Yosemite Falls, Mariposa Grove, and the Merced River Meadows in one day.

For a two-day visit, tour the valley floor, then leave for Mariposa Grove and for Glacier Point. If you have time, walk to Mirror Lake. When near Wawona, go to the Pioneer Yosemite History Center. This center is a collection of nine historical buildings and, during the summer, it is the setting for a living history program. There are music workshops, concerts, and dances. Other activities include stagecoach rides and nightly campfire programs.

Visitors are in for a treat when they visit Glacier Point. It offers some of the best *panoramas* of the valley and of the Sierra Nevada. Looking down

Water flows swiftly from Upper Yosemite Falls to Lower Falls.

Rafting on the Merced River is another way to enjoy Yosemite National Park.

from the stone overlook, tourists can view the Merced River—3,200 feet below!

Just across the valley is Yosemite Falls, Royal Arches, and Washington

FUN FACT Rock star David Lee Roth climbed Half Dome in Yosemite for pictures to be used on his "Skyscraper" album cover and in his music video.

Column. Vernal Fall and Nevada Fall are visible to the east. Up the Merced Canyon are the lofty peaks of the Sierra crest and Clark Range. Just think of all the pictures tourists have taken from this spot!

FUN FACT El Capitan is the world's largest exposed granitic monolith. It is equal in volume to four Rocks of Gibraltar.

THE LIFE ZONES OF YOSEMITE

In Yosemite National Park there are many kinds of fish, amphibians, reptiles, mammals, and birds. Not all of these are easily seen by visitors. However, each species contributes to the welfare of other plants and animals.

Animals stay within their life zones with their own communities of plants and animals. The elevation determines where they will live. Just what is a life zone? It is an area where there are identical types of plant and animal life and a single type of climate. A life zone can be compared to a layer. The plants and animals in one layer are different from the plants and animals in another layer.

Yosemite Valley's 4,000 foot elevation places it within the Transition Zone. Each clear day its northern walls are heated by the sun. The southern walls remain in shade and are always cool.

John Muir observed that all birds of the area knew the difference of weather between the two sides of the valley. The birds sought out the warmest nook on the north side to winter. In January the wrens, bluebirds, jays, and titmice were finding currants and laurel growing there. At the same time, across the valley on the south side, there was a blanket of snow.

The Yosemite region has five different life zones. The lowest life zone is the El Portal, Arch Rock area (500 to 3,000-4,000 feet). Tourists will see trees like toyon, mountain mahogany, and scrub oak. They'll see birds like the California thrasher, plain titmouse, and Bewick's wren. They'll see mammals like the brush rabbit, spotted skunk, and dusky-footed woodrat.

If tourists climb as high as they can, they'll reach the highest life zone. The Mount Dana and Lyell area is 11,000 to 11,500 feet above sea level. There hikers will see trees like the dwarf willow and various dwarf or matted flowering plants and turf-forming grasses and *sedges*. These are grasses that grow in wet places. Trees do not grow in this area. They'll see birds like the rosy finch and clark's nutcracker. They'll see mammals like the pika and marmot.

Flowering plants, grasses, and sedge grow on the highest areas of Yosemite.

FUN FACT Park rangers are asked: "What became of Half Dome's other half?" They answer: "The dome never had another half of solid rock. It only had slabs of granite on the sheer north face." These slabs were peeled away like an onion skin by advancing glaciers during the Ice Age.

TREES AND MEADOWS

Yosemite has three stands of *sequoias*. The largest is the world-famous Mariposa Grove with more than 500 mammoth trees. The Mariposa Grove is often called "Yosemite's Black Forest" because of its trees. The most photographed tree, the Wawona Tunnel Tree, was popular with visitors for many years because they could drive their cars through it. One day in February, 1969, however, it toppled under the weight of a record snowfall. It has been left where it fell.

Today the largest tree in the Mariposa Grove is the Grizzly Giant. It is hard to believe that this sequoia was once a tiny young seedling. It is 209 feet tall and 31 feet in diameter at its base.

Even a grown man looks small next to a sequoia tree.

The largest tree in Mariposa Grove is the "Grizzly Giant."

One day, a class of fifth-graders decided to see just how big the Grizzly Giant was. They joined hands around the tree. It took 27 students to do that. Then they joined hands around their school bus. That took only 18 students!

Just how the Grizzly Giant stands is one of the forest's mysteries. It has a definite lean. Most of the bark and sapwood at its base have been destroyed by fire. Once it was struck six times by lightning bolts in one storm! Yet the Grizzly Giant is still producing cones for new trees.

The largest meadow in the Sierra is Tuolumne Meadows, often called "Yosemite's Switzerland" because of its mountains. The area is usually snowed in seven months of the year. The best way to explore this high country's color and wildlife is by foot or on horseback.

The meadowlands are alive with wildflowers like Indian paintbrush, lupines, buttercups, wild geraniums, and shooting stars. They attract nectar-feeders like honey bees and bumblebees. They attract moths and butterflies.

In the meadow grass is a wonderful world of mosses, rare fungi, and small plants. Here live beetles, ants, and leafhoppers. It's a first-rate vacation spot for a *botanist* (a person who studies plants). It's also a great area for an *entomologist* (a person who studies insects).

Hodgdon Meadow is just inside the Big Oak Flat Entrance. It is near the famous Hetch Hetchy Reservoir, from which the city of San Francisco receives water and hydroelectric power.

DOMES AND WATERFALLS

Rising straight up at the west end of the valley floor is El Capitan. It is the world's largest *monolith* of exposed granite. A monolith is a solid, large block of stone. El Capitan has only a few cracks in its straight wall.

Half Dome is at the upper end of the valley. It looks like someone took a sharp knife and sliced it in half!

Half Dome, Sentinel Dome, and North Dome are results of a geologic process called *exfoliation* (scaling or peeling off in layers). Domes are solid rock shaped like gumdrops. Their roundness is the result of the granite shedding its outer layers, just as an onion sheds its many skins.

Other domes were formed differently. As the prehistoric ice flows melted and retreated, they rubbed enormous blocks of granite and polished domes like Liberty Cap, Lembert Dome, and Fairview Dome.

The solid block of stone known as "El Capitan" dominates the bank of the Merced River.

Nature shows off its many wonders throughout Yosemite National Park.

Nowhere in the world are there so many waterfalls in such a small area as in Yosemite. After the glaciers melted, small streams were left hanging high above the main valley floor. The streams formed steep waterfalls. They plunged into the deeper main valley.

Yosemite Falls is a typical example of this kind of waterfall. The Upper Yosemite Fall drops 1,430 feet. The Lower Yosemite Fall drops 320 feet. With the Middle Cascades drop of 675 feet—they have a combined height of 2,425 feet! This makes Yosemite Falls the highest waterfall in North America, and the fifth highest in the world. When tourists stand near Yosemite Falls, it sounds like a roaring volcano.

Bridalveil Fall spills over a long cliff four times the height of Niagara Falls. It is in the lower end of the valley. The fall has a 620-foot drop from its hanging valley.

With its many natural phenomena—sequoias, domes, meadows, and waterfalls, Yosemite has been called "Nature showing off!"

Yosemite's Half Dome looks like someone sliced a granite block in half.

WHAT'S TO DO BESIDES SIGHTSEE AT YOSEMITE?

Yosemite National Park is a place for family fun. There is something here for all ages. There are many things to do besides sightsee. Here are a few ideas:

Hike with the family. There are 800 miles of scenic trails. The going is tough, but the rewards are great. One of the more popular hikes is the Mist Trail that leads to Vernal and Nevada Falls. Another favorite is the loop around Mirror Lake. Happy Isles is the northern trailhead for the John Muir Trail.

Hike with a park ranger. You can learn about Yosemite by joining a nature walk. Rangers have studied the plants. They have learned about earth and rock formations in geology classes. Some may be experts on animal behavior. Rangers describe the history of the mountains and the people who lived and visited here. They tell about the flowers, trees, and vines.

Swim. Swim in the two swimming pools, one at Curry Village, the other at Yosemite Lodge. Or swim in the sparkling stream of the Merced River. But be careful. River swimming is not supervised, so you should never swim by yourself.

Ride a bicycle. You can bike eight miles of surfaced cycling paths. The trails are safe because they are separated from all car traffic. Ride the loop by Happy Isles. Another popular path is from Curry Village to Yosemite Lodge.

Fish! There are 200 lakes and 550 miles of streams open to tourists for fishing. The best place to catch fish is at Bridalveil Creek, Hetch Hetchy Reservoir, or Ten Lakes. There are five species of trout. Rainbow are the most numerous. You must purchase a California State fishing license to fish in Yosemite.

Go horseback riding. Rent one of the 400 horses at the four park stables. There are 635 miles of suitable trails, and if you're adventurous—try a High Sierra saddle trip.

Travel like Tom Sawyer. Rafting on the Merced River is ideal early in the summer when the water level and temperature are suitable. There is a three-and-one-fourth-mile stretch of smooth water that flows through the valley.

Bridalveil Falls spills over a cliff and into a deep, cool valley.

Some of Yosemite's waterfalls sound like roaring volcanoes.

It provides a relaxing way to see part of Yosemite Valley and Sentinal Dome. Tourists can canoe and kayak only on Tenaya Lake, Merced Lake, May Lake, and the Merced River between Lower Pines Campground and the El Capitan Bridge. Motors are prohibited on all boats.

Climb the rocks. People have been climbing in Yosemite since it was first settled. It's necessary to get professional training before starting to climb. Most climbing routes in the park are not for beginners. But there are many short climbs in the Tuolumne Meadows and Yosemite Valley. Cathedral Peak, Echo Peak, Mount Lyell, Cockscomb, and Matthes Crest are easier to climb. All climbers must register at the closest ranger station for any climb. Rescue teams need to know where to locate climbers if they do not return.

Enjoy the arts. Attend one of the free informal outdoor classes in painting. The four-hour sessions are taught by professionals. Visitors can try watercoloring, painting, sketching, or photographing the scenery.

There are also nature programs for children at the Happy Isles Nature Center. Many are planned for child and parent to do together.

One popular event is the Pony Picnic Ride. Children ride to the picnic site for songs, games, and a lunch. The parents walk and lead the ponies while the children ride along gentle bridle paths.

Bring a camera. Visit the Ansel Adams Gallery. Take one of the camera walks offered free. See the classic documentary film, *Ansel Adams: Photographer.*

The Yosemite Institute offers programs for learning about the natural and human history of the Sierra Nevada Mountains and Yosemite National Park. Their programs for students and adults offer a new understanding and appreciation of the outdoors.

Canoeists on Tenaya Lake can peacefully enjoy Yosemite.

Many animals make their home on and around Mirror Lake.

SEASONS AND WEATHER

Yosemite's scenery changes with the four seasons. In the Sierra Nevada, elevation affects the park's weather. Conditions can be different from one day to another. It can be spring in the lower foothills, while the higher elevations are still winterlike.

Tourists who visit in spring will usually find that the days are mostly mild and pleasant. Yosemite's thundering, tumbling waterfalls and descending cascades are fullest from the melting snow and runoff. Because of the force of this runoff, some waterfalls are unapproachable. Strong winds and sprays make a walk from the base of Yosemite Falls to the Yosemite Lodge an

exciting adventure.

In spring, the black oaks in Yosemite Valley begin to leaf out. Bears leave their dens with cubs. Mariposa lilies and numerous wildflowers paint the lower meadows. In the higher meadows, large blue lupines and yellow wallflowers are prominent.

Tourists who visit in summer will find that the days are about 15 hours long! This is wonderful for tourists who want to take advantage of all the outdoor activity in the park.

Temperatures in Yosemite Valley can reach 100°F. In Tuolumne Meadows, it can be 70°F in the daytime. At night, campers will want to snuggle in a woolen blanket or warm sleeping bag as the temperature slides down to the 30s. Summer skies sometimes give way to sudden downpours, flashes of lightning, noisy thunder, and gusty winds.

Spring arrives in July in the high country. It lasts only seven to nine weeks. But during those weeks, the entire upper meadows are dabbed with cheerful colors from blooming plants.

Tourists who visit in autumn will find that daytime temperatures are warm (but keep a sweater unpacked for the cooler nights). The sun's lower angle changes the surface of the granite domes. This makes them stand out and appear to move closer to the viewer.

Tourists who visit in winter will find that the weather is surprisingly mild. Day temperatures can reach the upper 40s to mid-60s. There are ten hours of daylight between dawn and dusk for tourists to enjoy a great many of the winter sports in the park.

Yosemite Valley receives an average of 29 inches of snow. Fortunately, the valley is sheltered by the height of the granite walls so it is not buried under snow.

The first snow in Tuolumne Meadows usually comes in November. Sometimes it can be ten or more feet deep in the high country. High passes, narrow passages between mountains, are closed off. Storm after storm buries the grasslands beneath the snow.

Visiting amateur and professional photographers can capture the glass-like coated twigs, the iced branches, and the frosted firs.

In autumn in the Yosemite Valley, the weather is cooler but the scenery is still beautiful.

The breathtaking Yosemite Valley is only a small part of Yosemite National Park.

BRACEBRIDGE CHRISTMAS DINNER PAGEANT

Christmas week is a popular time in Yosemite. The Bracebridge Christmas dinner pageant, held each year at the Ahwahnee Hotel, has become a tradition for thousands of Americans. This seven-course holiday meal is a tradition that began shortly after the hotel opened in 1927.

The Bracebridge ceremony is taken from descriptions in Washington Irving's "Sketch Book" of a Christmas Day in 1718 at Squire Bracebridge's Old English Manor. The dinner pageant takes four hours and involves more than 100 people in a theater production.

The meal draws more than 10,000 reservation requests from people all over the country. They want to spend the holiday in Yosemite. Only 1,800 of those 10,000 people who apply can be guests of the hotel during the five dinner seatings of 360 diners each! These meals are served on the afternoon and evening of December 22nd, Christmas Eve, and the afternoon and evening of Christmas Day.

TAKING CARE IN THE PARK

When you visit Yosemite, you should be cautious about certain things. For instance:

Swimming and water sports can be dangerous in mountain streams, or in lakes with a strong wind. Swim with a buddy.

Stream, river, and lake water may be unsafe to drink due to a protozoan that causes an intestinal disorder. Drink only tap water.

If a bear approaches, keep a safe distance. Do not tease or give food to a bear. Black bears consider anything they can smell food. They can smell humans!

Don't feed deer. Many seem tame. But they can be wild and unpredictable. Some are capable of causing serious injury and death.

Never travel alone. Campers should tell someone where they are going when they go for a hike.

FUN FACT For over 50 years, Ansel Adams took pictures of the Western landscapes, many in Yosemite. To honor him, in 1985 an 11,900-foot peak in Yosemite was named Mount Ansel Adams.

Horses and mules have the right-of-way on all trails. Hikers should step to the uphill (inside) edge of the trail. Remain quiet while the animals pass.

If tourists remember the park's rules, their visit can be full of fun and adventure. Yosemite National Park can be enjoyed by everyone all year round.

The Ahwahnee Hotel hosts a yearly Christmas dinner celebration.

FUN FACT Yosemite has a Junior Snow Ranger program. You can earn a certificate by attending any outdoor interpretive program.

A jeffrey pine tree grows firmly on top of Sentinel Dome in Yosemite National Park.

FOR MORE PARK INFORMATION

For more information about Yosemite National Park, write to:

National Park Service
Park Information Office
Box 577
Yosemite, CA 95389

Yosemite Park and Curry Company
5410 E. Home Avenue
Fresno, CA 93727

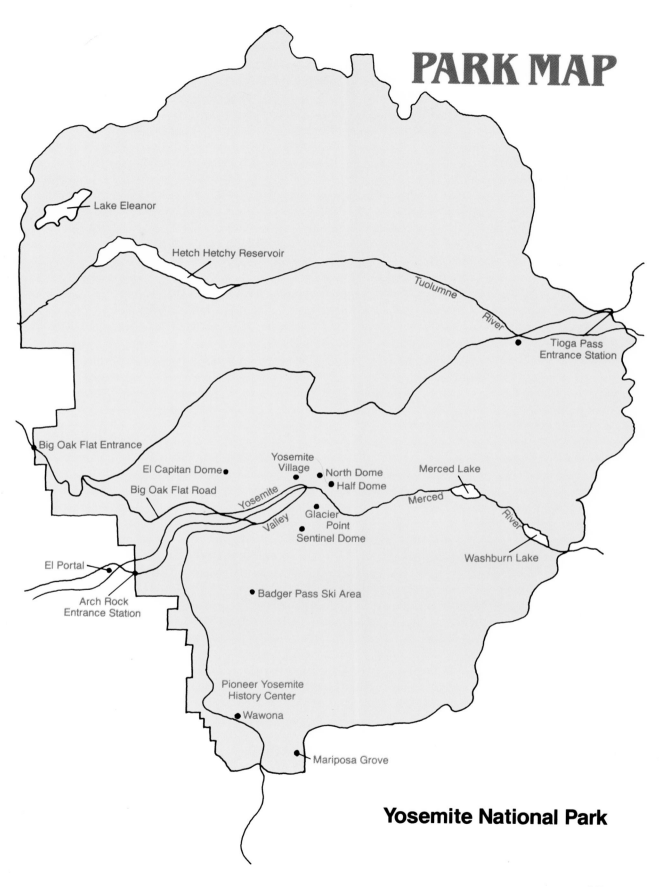

Lake Eleanor

Hetch Hetchy Reservoir

Tuolumne

River

Tioga Pass
Entrance Station

Big Oak Flat Entrance

El Capitan Dome

Yosemite
Village

North Dome

Half Dome

Merced Lake

Big Oak Flat Road

Yosemite

Merced

Valley

Glacier
Point

Sentinel Dome

River

Washburn Lake

El Portal

Arch Rock
Entrance Station

Badger Pass Ski Area

Pioneer Yosemite
History Center

Wawona

Mariposa Grove

Yosemite National Park

GLOSSARY/INDEX